MW00810132

Table of Contents

Puzzle Progress

Preparing for your professional career can often be a daunting experience. Some might say that this even feels like a puzzle.

Today, so many notifications are asking for our attention and there is so little awareness of our intentions. This lack of intentionality is why **52% of students are not confident they know how to find the right career path** [according to a Forage study in 2023]. Without knowing what career path to take, it is very difficult to take the steps to prepare. This is why **47% of college students don't feel career-ready** [according to a Forage study in 2023]. Career opportunities come from professional networks. But, few people are taught how to make intentional connections. This is why **58% of college students feel that they lack the necessary networking skills** [according to a World Metrics study in 2024]. Few people are intentional with budgets. This is why **88% of adults said, "high school did not leave them prepared for handling money"** [according to Ramsey Solutions 2023].

Within these pages, are the tools everyone should know, but few are taught.

Finding your suitable and fulfilling career requires a strategic approach beyond just landing any job. This workbook will guide you to be intentional in your steps so you will be **confident about your career path.**
You will be equipped to build a resume, cover letter, and have a stellar interview. After filling in the application section you will be **career ready.**
This workbook will teach you how to build a LinkedIn and give you tips on how to practice **necessary networking skills.**
Having a fulfilling life requires intentionality in how you spend your time and finances. After filling in the application section you will be **prepared for handling money.**

Remember, your journey is uniquely you! This workbook is designed to support you every step of the way. Let's get started and put your puzzle pieces together!

Direction

The First Piece

Everyone's life heads in a direction. Few people pick their direction intentionally.

You will only have some answers about where you want to end your career. That's okay; life is a journey. But make sure you embark on a journey that will be fulfilling for you. If you consider your passions and natural skills, you can make sure the experiences you pursue lead you in the direction that will be most interesting to you.

It can be overwhelming to determine the direction you want your career path to take. But there are a few simple components.

Start with the question:
1)"Who are you?" and use the Myers Briggs as a tool of self-reflection and awareness of your strengths, weaknesses, and career takeaways.

The second question is:
2)"Where are you now?" This helps assess your education and career experience as a starting point and for being proud of your accomplishments.

The final question is:
3)"Where are you interested in going?" You will look at your passions, skills, and experience here. This section will also provide some encouraging perspective for your journey!

Who are you?

Personality assessments are an easy way to understand who you are. The Myers-Briggs personality test provides an approach with 16 different personalities based on 5 categories. Tests like Myers-Briggs do not define your personality; instead, consider it a **tool** for understanding yourself.

A personality test is not a rulebook you must follow after knowing your type. It is more like a **mirror**. The purpose is to use the test to see within yourself and understand why you operate as you do.

Proceed through the QR code and find out about your personality! Once you have completed the test, view the next page to see that you have filled out your personality section.

Exercise Model

Circle the following sections that are related to you:

Extraverted or Introverted
Intuitive or Observant
Thinking or Feeling
Judging or Perceiving
Assertive or Turbulent

These represent your 5 categories: energy, mind, nature, tactics, and identity

My Personality is:

INTJ-A The Architect

My Strengths are:

- Rational
- Independent
- Determined

My Weaknesses are:

- Arrogant
- Combative
- Socially Clueless

Only write the things that you find relatable to yourself

My Career Paths and Workplace Habits are:

I prefer roles that offer me independence. I tend to be happier in roles that allow me to innovate in big or small ways.

Titles do not matter that much to me and I may find it hard to avoid giving feedback and criticism to my superiors

My Key Takeaway is:

Knowledge and my brain are key aspects of my personality and work life

Exercise

Circle the following sections that are related to you:

Extraverted or Introverted

Intuitive or Observant

Thinking or Feeling

Judging or Perceiving

Assertive or Turbulent

My Personality is:

My Strengths are:

✦

✦

✦

My Weaknesses are:

✦

✦

✦

My Career Paths and Workplace Habits are:

My Key Takeaway is:

Where are you?

Now that you know your personality better, shift your perspective to where you are professionally. It is crucial to understand where your journey begins to **find the direction** you wish to go.

Exercise Model

Education level:

Freshman at Smallville Community College

Current job position[s]:

Cashier at Jack-in-the-Box

Volunteer at my church

Circle which statements apply to you:

Working on my degree

Working on my career

Working on myself [gap year]

Working on my business

Working on a trade

I don't know yet

At this stage, it is okay to not know where you are.

Which describes you best?

I know what's next

What is happening??

I'm along for the ride

Exercise

Education level:

Current job position(s):

Circle which statements apply to you:

Working on my degree

Working on my career

Working on myself (Gap year)

Working on my business

Working on a trade

I don't know yet

Which describes you best?

I know what's next

What is happening??

I'm along for the ride

Think Ahead

It is okay not to know where you are! It is often something you do not actively assess. Figure out where you want to go and establish your starting point. Work backwards.

Where Do You Want To Go?

Passion

Not all your passions need to be a professional pursuit, but it helps if you are interested in learning about your work.

Being passionate about your industry can make your work feel **purposeful** and **exciting**! What kind of work are you passionate about doing?

Not all your passions need to be a professional pursuit

What are you passionate about? List your passions and interests below:

Think about things that you enjoy doing and make you happy: Videogames, Reading, Making lists, Chemistry, etc.

Skillset

What are you good at? Is there something that **comes naturally** to you or feels like it clicks? This does not have to be math, science, writing, or language. Put simply: What makes sense to you?

List 5-10 skills you are good at. These can be hard skills like computer programs, industry skills, or subject knowledge. They can also be soft skills like time management, organization, or leadership.

1 __________
2 __________
3 __________
4 __________
5 __________
6 __________
7 __________
8 __________
9 __________
10 __________

Looking Ahead:
Discover what you are skilled at now so that when you reach your application phase, you can play to your key strengths

Experience

If you have some experience, that's fantastic! Reflect on how that experience (what you now know about an industry) is beneficial.

What have you learned from your past experiences?

If you need experience, then this is the perfect time to get started!

Experience

Just Try It. Pick an industry you think you would like to work in. Get an entry-level job in that industry to try it out.

What are a few entry-level jobs you could "just try" to see if this is what you thought & what you like?

After you try a new job you can reflect on whether this position is something you want to pursue, or not. Either way, be proud of yourself for the gained experience!

I Liked It.
Great! Stick with it! Concentrate on jobs in the same industry which will compound your tacit knowledge and skill set to make you an expert.

I Didn't Like It.
That is completely okay! Now you know you need to pivot your trajectory and do not want to pursue a career in that field.

Professional Trifecta

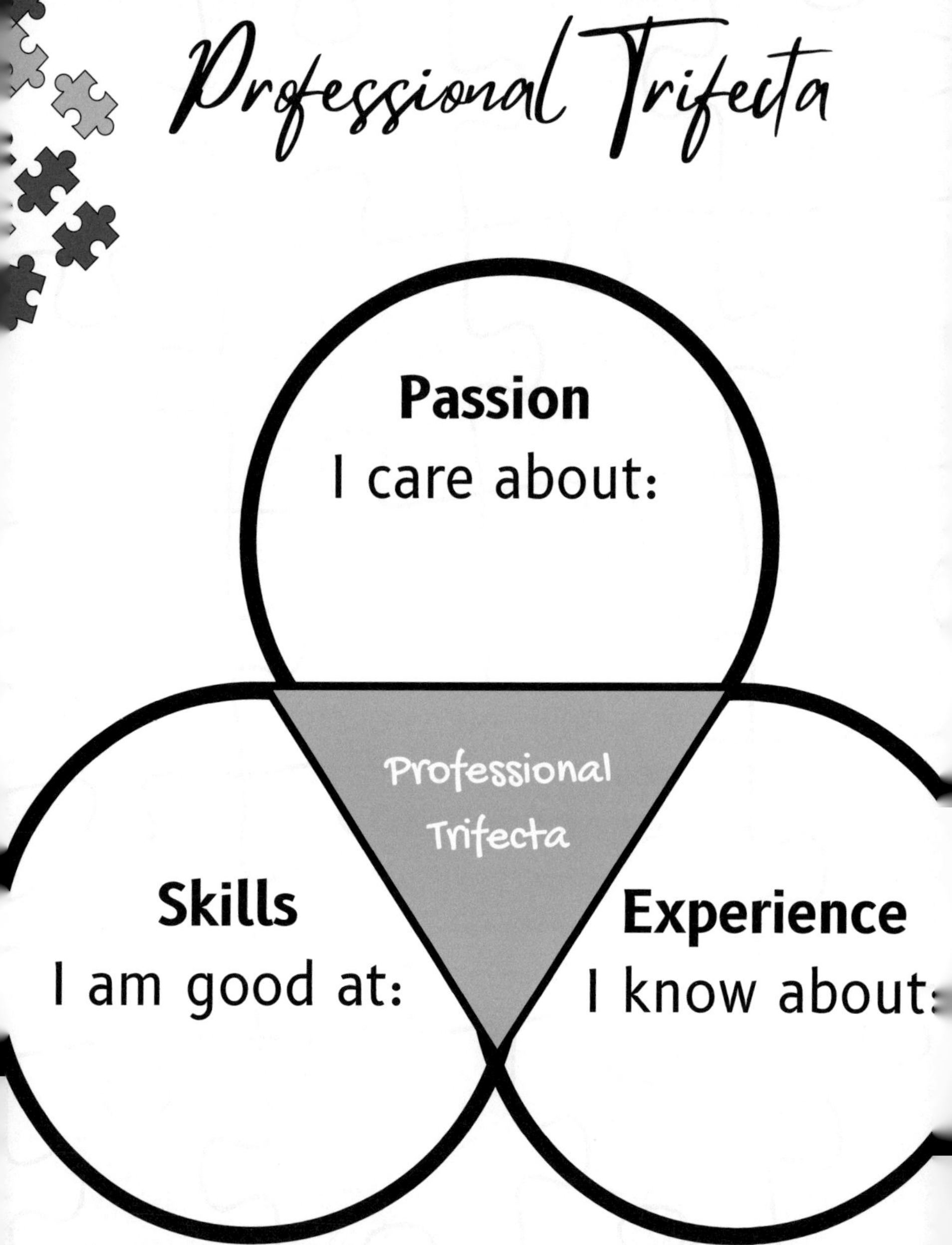

Often, you can find your stride when your experience, passion, and skills align. When these three align with each other, you have a starting point that can drive your end goals.

Professional Trifecta

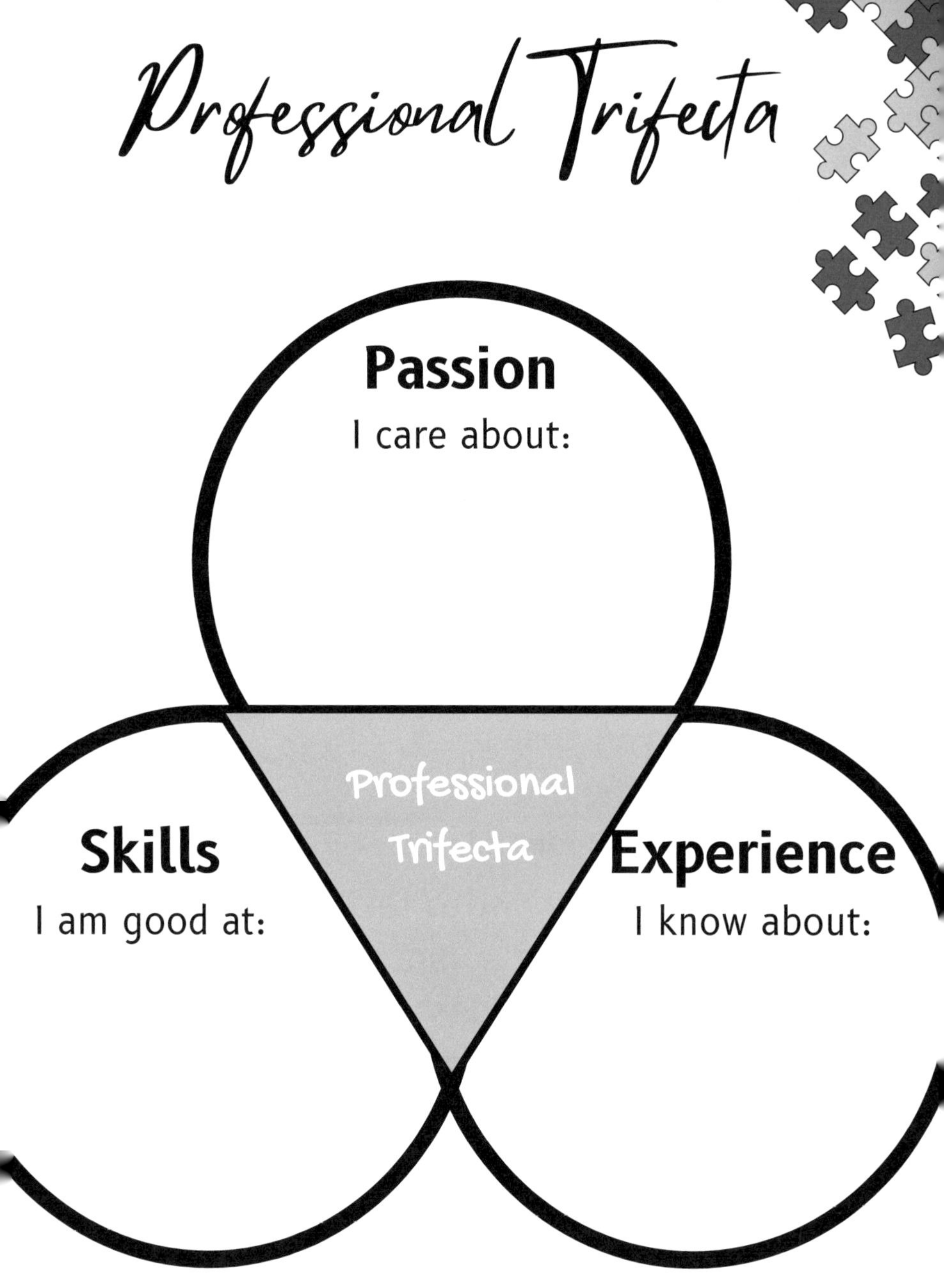

Fill in your Professional Trifecta!
[*pull from previous pages*]

Perspective for the Journey

Waste of Time. If you spend time looking into an option and realize that is not the direction you are passionate about, that was not a waste of time. A waste of time would be to never get started and try. A waste of time would be to stick with something you do not care about because you never looked into other options. It is an answer in itself that the option you were looking into is not the one you want to take. Sometimes, you try to push a puzzle piece into place, but it does not fit. That does not mean the puzzle piece is a failure and should be thrown away. It will still be a valuable part of the whole picture. It was just being pushed into the wrong place. It belongs somewhere else where it will be a better fit.

> *A waste of time would be to never getting started.*

Failure. Do not let your fear of failure stop you from getting started. Redefine your goal to **learning**. Learn about your job, industry, the process, a new skill, what you like, and what you are not passionate about. If your goal is to learn and not on the outcome of success, you will not fail.

How does your fear of failure hold you back?

Redefine your goals so they are *not* about an outcome you will fail or achieve. Redefine your goals to what you *could* learn in the process:

In the space below, write *three* career learning goals.

1.

2.

3.

BE brave

Low-Risk Learning. Experiment when the stakes are low. If you are embarking on your professional journey or "adult life," this is your moment. The more "anchors" you have later in life (spouse, kids, pets, house, car, payments), the more your stability matters. But if you are untethered and can swing for the fences, go for it. Experimenting with low stakes allows us the "freedom to fail." "What if I start at that job and hate it?" You could get a new one. "What if I move there and don't like it?" You can always move back. "What if I am not good at teaching yoga?" You will get better. Just try it; what is the worst thing that can happen? You start over? So what?

Whether or not you have "anchors," you can always grow through low-risk learning. Try a job in a field you are curious about. Practice a hobby or skill. The more you can practice learning and experimenting on your own time, the more you will have techniques you feel comfortable with in your tool belt.

Think Ahead:

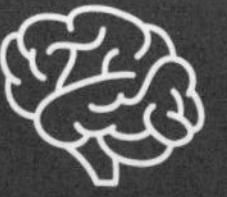

What could you experiment with and learn about while the stakes are low?

Self-efficacy is the belief that you are capable enough. It is how "effective you believe yourself to be." It is the ability to believe in oneself. When you take advantage of opportunities, amazing things happen. This positive effect is cyclical; hence, it's called the **Self-Efficacy Cycle**.

1] The more opportunities you **apply** for, the more you will learn. If you get the job, excellent! If you didn't, you have more practice interviewing, learning how to present yourself, and more about the company you researched.

2] The more opportunities you take, the more you will **grow**. These experiences will give you more skills.

3] These new skills will allow you to believe that you are capable. This increased **confidence** will be attractive as you apply for new opportunities.

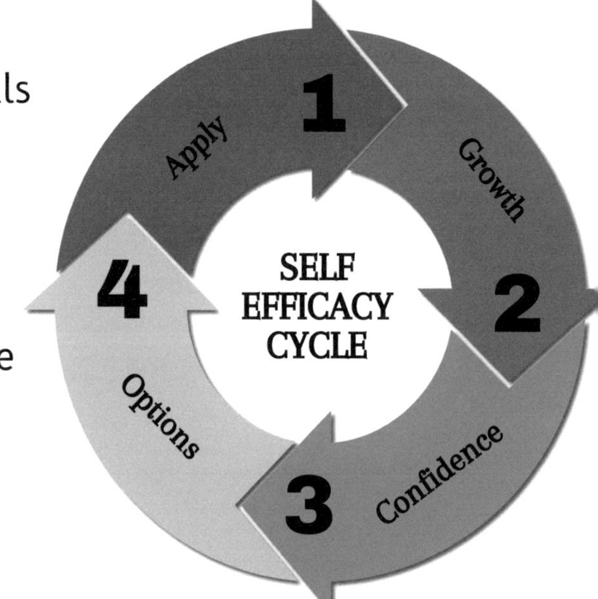

4]The more opportunities you apply for, the less you need each individual one. Have you ever noticed yourself drawn to secure people and repelled by desperate people? Knowing someone has other **options** makes them more attractive. It means different people see value in them, too, and if they decide to work for you, it is because they want to, not because it is their only choice and they have to. Be someone with options. Utilize all your opportunities and apply for new ones.

When you go to apply for these options you will have a higher degree of self-efficacy [believing yourself to be effective] since you have had more experiences where you applied yourself, grew, and gained confidence! You know you can do this since you have succeeded in the past.

Where are you at in your journey on the self-efficacy cycle? How could you reach the next step? Jot down some of your ideas:

I am at the

I can reach the next step by doing:

✦

✦

✦

Journey. Enjoy it. It might feel like you are directionless or utterly lost, but if you take the steps in this workbook, you are much closer to putting the whole picture together than you think. One day, you may look back and think about this grind time to try to figure it out. It was part of the good old days. Please remember that everyone's journey is going to look different because we have all been given pieces to different puzzles, and no puzzle is going to fit together that same way. That is part of the adventure of it! You are uniquely and wonderfully made, and your finished puzzle will fit together in a unique and wonderful way. Just keep putting pieces down, one at a time, and eventually, it clicks and builds a whole picture.

Destination. Sometimes, it is easier to know where you want to end up than how to get there. So we can look backward. When you think about your future, what would have to be in place for you to think, "I did it."

What would it take to be settled and content? What destination has value to you?

You know who you are!
You know where you are!
You know where you want to end up!

Application

The Second Piece

You can bring value to this company. It's time to show them why.

Applying for a job requires writing a resume, a cover letter, and an interview. These three elements may seem foreign and separate from one another, but success comes when you understand that they overlap significantly. If you know your career journey, experience, and the company you want to work for, you can use the resume, cover letter, and interview to prove why you are the perfect fit for any position.

Application

It can be overwhelming to apply for jobs. This process has many steps, including a resume, cover letter, and interview. When you truly understand the components, all these steps will build on one another.

Start with the question:
1] "What is your career journey?" Focus on explaining your direction. This is the journey from where you started to where you want to end up.

The second question is:
2] "What have you done?" Your career experience will help prove why you are prepared to be an asset in any company.

The final question is:
3] "What company do you want to work for?" Understanding the company will help you market yourself as a candidate who would fulfill the company's needs.

25 What is Your Career Journey?

Let's begin crafting your story:

Keep all of this in mind, we will return to it later

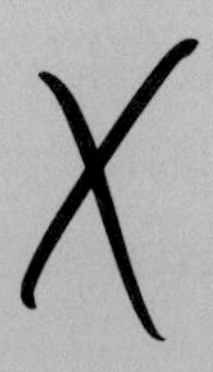

Start with where you are at [**A**]. This is where the alphabet and your journey begin. Reflect back to Direction and think about *who you are* and *where you are.*

Next, focus on the experience [**X**]. This is designed to have you focus on what you have done. The Resume acts as a crucial guide in storytelling.

Y

Now for the "why?" [**Y**]. Explain why your experience is important. Think about how you can apply your "A" and "X" to your career goals.

End with your destination [**Z**]. This is your desired end goal. Reflect back on Direction and see *where you want to end up.*

Write A Resume

Resume. This document is the pinnacle of the application process. So what is it? A resume is essentially a one-page extended summary of your work history. The goal is to be specific and detailed about the skills you utilized through your work experiences. A resume will include your contact information, education, work, leadership, and/or volunteer experience sections. The main emphasis in the resume will be the experience sections, as it is most crucial in defining the experience (X) variable of your story.

So how do you write it? There is no one way to do a resume. Plenty of templates exist out there, but the best way to start is by creating it yourself. This is the only way you can ensure your resume will not look like anyone else's. There are four key sections that every resume will need to include:

1. Header
2. Education
3. Experience
4. Skills

Look Ahead

There is plenty of information to potentially include, but keep everything to ONE page.

Resume Model

Header

The Header is simple. All you need is your name and contact information.

John Doe

jdoe@gmail.com | [343] 564-8777 | Smallville, Big State

Education

This is another easy section. All you need is the name of your school/college, the title of your degree or diploma, and your graduation year.

Smallville Community College April. 2025
Associate of Arts in Communication Sciences

Experience

Your experience section is the most vital section on your resume. This is where you explain your experience [X] through bullet points. It will include the company name, job title, dates of involvement, and 3-4 bullets about the experience.

Joe's Famous Restaurant May 2022 - Present
Host

- Greet 100 customers daily to create a welcoming environment within the restaurant

Hard Skills

Your hard skills will be any sort of computer programs, relevant certifications, or languages you may speak. Do not include soft skills like time management or leadership.

Resume Practice

Fill out the following with applicable information:

Education

School Name:

Degree/Diploma:

Graduation Year:

Experience

Company Name:

Your Job Title:

Dates:

Bullet Points are the trickiest part of the resume. You really want to highlight your experience well. So, for this section, just practice the basics. Simply state, in 2-3 words, what you did in the role.

Example: Took orders

You will workshop these later

Hard Skills

It's okay if you do not have any of these, yet!

Computer Programs:

Certifications:

Languages:

Bullet Point Workshop

The key to any experience section is highlighting your specific skillset. A resume has a one-page limit, so you can use bullet points to state your accomplished tasks.

To write a bullet point, start with a verb and add specific metrics. Specific metrics could be the number of customers, $ amount, number of employees, events, etc. It allows the recruiter to see the scope of your task. Also, add reasoning to answer the "why" or "how" you did the task.

Joe's Famous Restaurant May 2022
Host

- ~~Customer Service~~
- **Greeted 100 customers** daily to create a welcoming environment within the restaurant
- ~~Cashier~~
- **Managed** a cashbox of **$200** and maintained financial responsibility while taking orders and giving change
- ~~Managed team~~
- **Directed 24 employees,** which included delegating tasks and conducting performance reviews regularly

Bullet Point Workshop

Return to your resume exercise and look at your experience section. Now that you know a little bit more about writing resume bullet points, start with those 2-3 words and expand to form a whole point.

Bullet Points

Started With: Took orders

Changed To: Took and assembled 50+ orders daily in an efficient manner to guarantee timely service and customer satisfaction

This is your "x"

Started With:

Changed To:

Started With:

Changed to:

Think Ahead

When you write bullet points, make sure that they are relevant to the job or company you are applying for.

Resume Checklist

As you begin creating your own resume, use this sheet as a guide to help you keep track of the necessary content.

1 **Header Section:**

- [ ] Name | Contact Information

2 **Education Section:**

- [ ] School name | Graduation Year
- [ ] Full Degree/Diploma Title

3 **Professional Experience Section:**

- [ ] Organization name | Year
- [ ] Full Position Title
- [ ] 3-4 Bullet Points (X)

4 **Hard Skills Section:**

- [ ] Computer Software
- [ ] Certifications
- [ ] Languages

only add these if they are applicable

Resume Template

Full Name

Professional Email | Phone Number | City, State

Education

Full University Name Year

Full Degree Title

Professional Experience

Organization Name Year

Full Position Title

- Description of job task
- Description of job task

Organization Name Year

Full Position Title

- Description of job task
- Description of job task

Skills

Computer Software | Certifications | Language

Write a Cover Letter

Cover Letter. Cover Letters are typically tricky for first-time writers. You need to refer to two documents. So, when you begin a cover letter, grab the job description from the company's job posting and your resume. Take the job description and look for what they want from their potential hire. Look at your resume and see where there is overlap and transferable experience. That transferable experience [X] is the focal point in your cover letter.

Boiled down, the cover letter is essentially a response to the job description. The company is saying, "This is who we are looking for...," and your response is, "This is how I am who you are looking for."

> *"The cover letter is essentially a response to the job description"*

You are connecting the dots for the company and showing them why you are interested in their position and how you'd be an asset to them. The cover letter, in many ways, is like a pre-interview.

35 Do Your Company Homework

Before you begin writing your cover letter, you need to understand the company, which adds a new variable:

"**C**" represents the company. To write a cover letter, you must understand the audience you are writing to. The best way to do that is by researching the company and job before you begin.

Here are the most important components to research in order to be prepared to write your cover letter and conduct your interview:

- Job description
- Company mission statement
- What products / services do they offer?
- Observations from the company website
- Observations from company social media
- Why do you like this company?

If you have this information, you know what matters to that company. Then, you can explain your story and experience in a way that will be most meaningful to that company.

Do Your Company Homework

Company Research

Pick a company you are interested in and practice your research. Take simple notes below:

Job Description:

Company Mission Statement:

Products / Services:

Company Website Take Aways:

Company Social Media Take Aways:

What Do You Like About Their Company?

Cover Letter Checklist

Use this document as a way to organize your thought process as you go about writing your cover letter.

1 **Header Section:**

- [ ] Name | Contact Information
- [ ] Dear "__________"

2 **Interest Section:**

"C" is a new variable, but it just represents any company information.

- [ ] [C] Company Itself
- [ ] [C] Company Position

3 **Value Section:**

This is your resume bullet points

- [ ] [X] Experience
- [ ] [Y] Why is that helpful?
- [ ] [C] Tie back to company

4 **Anticipatory Section:**

- [ ] Thank you for your time
- [ ] Looking forward to next steps
- [ ] Sincerely,

Cover Letter Template

Full Name

Professional Email | Phone Number | City, State

Dear _______________,

If you do not know who you are writing to, put "Hiring Manager"

Interest Paragraph [C]

Discuss why you are interested in the company and the position being offered.

Value Paragraph [X & Y]

Briefly explain your experience [X] that has prepared you be of valuable to the company. Explain why [Y] this experience makes you valuable and why you want to work for that company [C].

Anticipatory Paragraph

Thank them for their time. Express your positive anticipation about the next steps in the process.

Sincerely,

____

You can add a handwritten signature here if you'd like

Cover Letter Practice

Value Paragraph Practice

Take the company and job you picked from the Company Research Homework and practice writing about your value.

Company You Chose: ______________________

Job You Are Applying For: ______________________

What do you bring to the table? Think about the resume and pull 2-3 skills this company would find valuable for the job your applying for.

This is your "X" variable

1. ______________________
2. ______________________
3. ______________________

Why do the above skills matter to that company? Why should those skills qualify you to work for that company? Explain *one* of your skills and why it makes you an asset to the company in 2-3 sentences below.

This is your "Y" variable

Reflection

Remember this table? You haven't seen it for a few pages, but now you're ready to fill it out.

Start with where you are at [**A**]. This is where the alphabet and your journey begin. Reflect back to Direction and think about *who you are* and *where you are*.

Next, focus on the experience [**X**]. This is designed to have you focus on what you have done. The Resume acts as a crucial guide in storytelling.

Now for the "why?" [**Y**]. Explain why your experience is important. Think about how you can apply your "A" and "X" to your career goals.

End with your destination [**Z**]. This is your desired end goal. Reflect back on Direction and see *where you want to end up*.

Story Crafting Model

Return to previous pages, grab information, and pull it here to this table!

Go back to your Direction section and see what you put down under "Who I Am" and "Where I Am." Jot down some of your ideas in the space provided below:

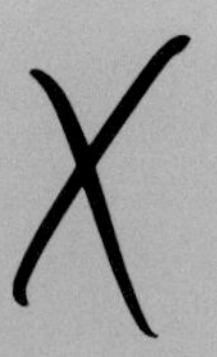

Look at your resume and cover letter sections. What skills have you gained from past experiences? What experience do you have? Jot them down here:

Story Crafting Model

Return to previous pages, grab information, and pull it here to this table!

y

Consider the "why" of your experiences. Why are they important? Why do they matter to the company you are applying for? Put your "whys" below:

This is the final destination. What is it that you want? Reflect back on your Direction chapter and see where you set that goal. Bring that information here:

The Interview Process

Interview. Interviewing tends to be the dreaded aspect of the job process. It is the pinnacle of all of your preparation. A resume, cover letter, application, and your connections all funnel down into this interview. It is a big deal, but you won't go in unprepared!

Sample Questions. Practicing ahead of time will help you think through your work experience at home, so when you are in the interview, you can explain your experience concisely and feel confident in your answer.

It is crucial not to memorize word for word answers. Word for word answers can feel over rehearsed and insincere. Instead, focus on your stories and examples so the wording is still fresh and your main points are top of mind when you answer.

Practice Questions

Tell me about yourself. The elevator pitch is the inevitable interview question asked as the opener to start the conversation. The key here is to be conversational. You can 1] share your "*A*" to "*Z*." Give them an idea of where you started or are at and where the end goal is. 2] Share a bit about what makes you unique and relevant to your interests without being too personal.

Add your highlights from the Story Crafting Model that reflect your A and Z in the space below.

What makes you unique? Think about your skillset related to the position you are applying for. [Use your Professional Trifecta.] List a few ideas here.

Practice Questions

Strengths and Weaknesses. Interviewers want to hear your thoughts about yourself and the value you can add to their team. Prepare for these questions by conducting a self-analysis. Then use examples from career experience.
Use the Tell and Show model to help you plan how to answer these questions. Talk about the skill and then explain how you have utilized it in a previous experience.

What is your biggest strength?

Share the trait that is unique to you and will make you an asset for this role. This is the time to advocate for yourself. Jot some story starters below.

This is your strength

Tell: high order of initiative

Show: self-starting a class project that led to meeting the deadline early and increasing academic efficiency overall

This is how you used it

Tell:

Show:

Tell:

Show:

Practice Questions

What is your biggest weakness? Give a lot of thought to this question.

1] You need to give an answer that feels sincere, but...

2] You also do not want to paint yourself as an unemployable candidate. So tell them a weakness and follow it up with how you are working on it to be more well-rounded.

In the space below, fill in your weakness and how you are improving in that area.

This is your weakness

Tell: I am not naturally gifted at organization

Show: so, now I use a planner to be more diligent in this area

This is how you are working to change

Tell:

Show:

Tell:

Show:

Look Ahead

Some weaknesses are not authentic weaknesses. "**Perfectionism**" or being "**too detail-oriented**" are not weaknesses. Do not pose strengths as weaknesses. Be genuine and show a weakness with how you are improving in that area.

Practice Questions

Tell me about a time you had a conflict with a coworker and how you resolved it. Same idea here: specific, sincere example, and follow it up with how you made amends and what that taught you.

Fill in the model below:

This is the conflict

This is the resolution

Tell: My coworker and I closed the store differently,

Show: so, I asked her why she did tasks in a certain order and what she thought worked well, so we could coordinate our efforts better and work as a team.

Tell:

Show:

Why do you want this job / to work here? Slam dunk! You already have these answers written down on your Company Research Homework on page 36.

Bring those "whys" and bullet them here:

-
-
-
-

Practice Questions

Out-of-the-Box Questions. Although not always common, be prepared to think critically about yourself. Your answer does not actually matter, but your thinking does. Interviewers want to see that you can solve problems and provide persuasive reasoning.

Use the space below to practice your reasoning when asked an abstract question.

Abstract Question Example: What kind of kitchen utensil would you be?

Unimportant Answer: A mixing spoon

Vital Reasoning: They are used in a batter to mix many different elements and flavors into one dish.

Relevance to Real Life: When I work with a team, I help my coworkers mix elements of their strengths to be more efficient.

Abstract Question Example: What school material would you be?

Unimportant Answer:

Vital Reasoning:

Relevance to Real Life:

Think Ahead

Although you may not be asked abstract questions in every interview, the process is still important to practice your reasoning skills.

Apply For The Job

Have Work Evidence Ready to Go. Think about the skills/projects listed in the job description and your previous work experience that has prepared you for this role or shows aspects of what you can do.
[Videos, photos, reviews, statistics, attendance numbers, sales, etc.]

Make it "ready to go" by printing it, putting it on your desktop in a folder, pulling the website up on your computer, or placing it on your phone in a new album. This will save you the embarrassing moment of scrolling through your camera roll for too long while the interviewer waits.

What work evidence could you have "ready to go?"

✦ ________________________________

If you don't have any yet, that's okay!

✦ ________________________________

✦ ________________________________

✦ ________________________________

Attire. Here are a few tips! When coming to an interview, consider dressing to show your potential employer that you would fit into their company culture. If you are applying for a surf apparel company, you may consider wearing something from their brand and being dressed less formally. If you were applying for an investment banking position, where the expectation is full professional attire; you would want to dress in business attire. With that in mind, err on the side of professionalism. It never hurts to be the "best dressed in the room," it is far better to be too formal than too casual. Dressing professionally shows you have responsibility and self-respect in the work you take on. Dressing too casually may show your employer you are not serious about the opportunity they are giving you. You are probably familiar with the famous phrase: "It is good to dress for the job you want, not the job you have."

> *"It is far better to be too formal than too casual."*

Apply For The Job

Body Language. Eye contact and body language are things one does not typically think of when it comes to interviews. Try to make eye contact when they are asking and you are answering questions. You do not have to stare at them the entire time; make it natural. You do not want to be looking down at your hands or above the interviewer's head. You are having a conversation with the person, so look at them. Also, making eye contact is a sign of respect in American culture.

Beyond just the skills and experience you demonstrate in an interview, your body also sends a message to the employer. Try not to fidget or twirl in a spinning chair. The bearing or posture you convey says a lot about the type of candidate you are. If you are slouching or lying back in the chair, you leave the interviewer to make assumptions about your personality and character. Sitting straight with your chin up and making eye contact demonstrates a confident posture that the interviewer can pick up on and appreciate.

Interview Checklist

The Story Crafting Model you completed on page 41 sets you up for your interview preparation.

1 Company Research

- [ ] page 36 of workbook

2 Dressed for Success

- [ ] Hygiene | Attire
- [ ] Punctual | Body Language

3 Know how to tell my story

- [ ] [A] Start
- [ ] [X] Experience
- [ ] [Y] Why
- [ ] [Z] Destination

4 Work Evidence Ready

- [ ] Specific Metrics
- [ ] Previous Projects

Hooray! You got the job! Now let's learn how you can *apply* yourself to the job.

Apply Yourself To The Job

Be Dependable. Being a dependable employee will often make you a promotable employee. It is hard for business owners and managers to find help who will care about their business as much as they do. It is strenuous for businesses to hire, train, and schedule employees. It will not go unnoticed if you are someone they can count on. This means:

- Show up early and clock in on time
- Dress fully in the required attire
- Bring any required materials
- Clock out for lunch breaks and at the end of shifts accurately
- Communicate your time off so supervisors, managers, and owners can make accommodations to cover your shift.

Think Ahead:

How can you begin preparing for your future job? Do you need to work on your time management skills?

Apply Yourself To The Job

Be Promotable. If you are in the industry or business you want to progress in, go the extra mile. Be the first one there and the last one to leave. Eventually, you will earn a reputation for being someone they can count on to fill in when something needs to get done. As that trust is built, your role will expand. As you learn about your industry and your company's process, people will ask you for answers and advice. You can learn the jobs of your teammates. This will allow you to:

- Help them when they are overwhelmed
- Cover for them if they cannot make it; your team needs that role filled.
- Expand your specialization with different skills and roles
- Extend your understanding of how the whole company machine operates.
- Ask questions about what others do, why they do it, and how it works. People love to feel knowledgeable; it will make their day when they tell you about their role and the motivation behind their decisions.

Apply Yourself To The Job

Team Work Makes The Dream Work. Help other people. Even when you do not see how it will benefit you. Cover for your team. Do the hard job. Support your group when they are struggling. Fill in where you can. It is incredible what a true team can do.

Looking out for the interests of others and celebrating each other's successes is just the tip of the iceberg for team potential. When a true team is formed, there is little they cannot accomplish. Strive to build this kind of team because being on one is worth it.

Your manager/boss will see that you are a team player. Your customers will see that you are a team player. Your suppliers will see that you are a team player. By showing that you are capable of working with a team, you demonstrate your ability to be dependable and promotable. Start working on your teamwork skills by:

- Caring about others
- Speaking well of others
- Being **genuine** in both professional and personal life

Applying Yourself. By applying yourself early on, it will make you successful in life and your career. Being able to articulate your career story from where you started at [*A*] to where you want to end up [*Z*] helps people understand your direction.

Explaining your experience [*X*] and why it's crucial [*Y*] allows employers to see the value you bring to the table.

Understanding the company [C] you want to work for allows you to describe how you fulfill their job description and company goals and how you can contribute to their company once you've been hired.

You understand your career journey!
You can explain your experience!
You did research on the company!

Application

Connection

The Third Piece

It's all about who you know.

You are going to interact with people; everyone does. But success comes from being the person who interacts and connects with people. Let them get to know you and your career journey, experience, and hopes. Get to know them. Listen to their goals and help them get there. This will organically build your network.

Connection

Networking can be intimidating. However, it can be done organically if you are intentional and professional in the relationships you will naturally build throughout your life and career.

Start with the question:
1]**"How can I build my LinkedIn?"** Utilize this digital platform as your online and more descriptive resume.

The second question is:
2]**"How can I build a network?"** Connecting on LinkedIn and organically in person are fantastic ways to build a network.

The final question is:
3]**"How can I maintain my network?"** Ensure you communicate consistently and keep track of your connections. This will allow you to maintain your network.

Building Your LinkedIn

LinkedIn is its own unique creature. Unlike other social media platforms, it has a strictly professional purpose. There are no memes or reels to give you a good laugh. LinkedIn requires an intentional and methodical approach. There are several key sections that you want to incorporate into your profile.

Story-Driven vs Task-Oriented.

When talking to a recruiter or sharing in an interview, start with a story driven approach and end a task-oriented approach. Your story will be whys and motivations behind what you are doing or why you have the goals you do. The story is about you; it's a narrative. The task-oriented side is what you did and how you did it. Tasks are about execution; "how did you accomplish this project?"

Visual Section. The visual section is the first impression recruiters will have when viewing your LinkedIn profile. This acts as your smile and "Hello!"

There are four components in the visual section: headshot, background, name, and tagline. The profile picture you include should be a professional business headshot. The background can be a simple image that is relevant to your industry. If your photos from your industry are not aesthetic, consider having a scenic photo as the background or an image related to your personal brand. Include your name as written on your resume. Lastly, add a tagline. Your tagline can be your major and career goal.

About Section. The first section is the "About" section. This section acts as the hook that gets a viewer to want to scroll down and learn more about you and your experience.

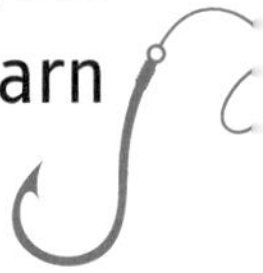

The goal of this section is to **share your story**. Give the reader an overview of your **past**. Explain what you have done in the past and why that matters to your growth?
Next, you should focus on your **present** and what you are pursuing and working towards. Lastly, close it with your goals for the **future** by highlighting what you hope to achieve. The About Section is very similar to aspects of the application process as it ultimately introduces you. If the Visual Section is a smile and "Hello!", the About Section is a firm handshake and an elevator pitch.

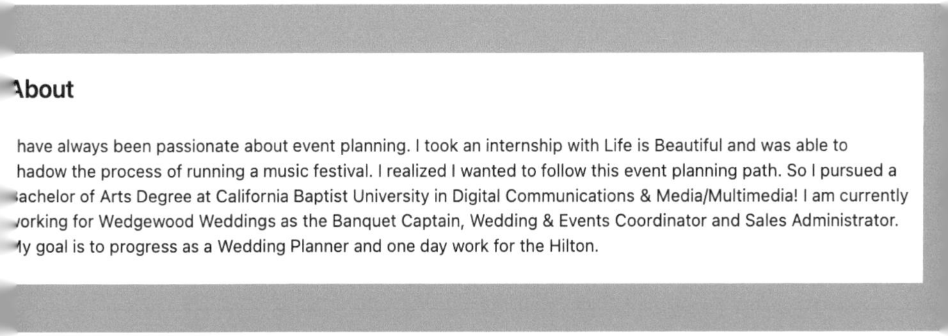

About

have always been passionate about event planning. I took an internship with Life is Beautiful and was able to hadow the process of running a music festival. I realized I wanted to follow this event planning path. So I pursued a achelor of Arts Degree at California Baptist University in Digital Communications & Media/Multimedia! I am currently orking for Wedgewood Weddings as the Banquet Captain, Wedding & Events Coordinator and Sales Administrator. ly goal is to progress as a Wedding Planner and one day work for the Hilton.

About Section Model

To craft your About Section, consider your Story Crafting Model on page 41.

What you did in the Past?

What have you already accomplished? On LinkedIn, you want to focus on where you started and have previously achieved. In your first paragraph (3-4 sentences) address your interests (relevant to your industry), and what you have already done.

What are you doing in the Present?

What are you doing right now? Are you in college or a certificate program? What are you currently working on? A degree, project, an internship, or a job? How does what you are working on contribute to your career pursuits? Write another 3-4 sentences illustrating these experiences and their importance.

What will you do in the Future?

Everything you have done and are doing culminates into the pinnacle which is your end goal. Why does your experience, past and present, matter to your career pursuit? How are you being prepared for the future?

Think Ahead:

Keep a consistent story between Application and Connection. A recruiter may look at both your resume and LinkedIn, so keep the narrative the same.

About Section Exercise

Use this exercise to create an outline for your About Section.

What you did in the Past?

In the space below, write down some of your most notable past experiences and accomplishments.

- ✦
- ✦
- ✦
- ✦

What are you doing in the Present?

What are you currently doing that points towards your career future? Write down those ideas here:

- ✦
- ✦
- ✦
- ✦

What will you do in the Future?

How do the past and present experiences contribute to your career goal? Write down your goal and how you hope to achieve it below:

Goal:

How will you achieve it:

Building Your LinkedIn

Education Section. This section is relatively simple when it comes to content. You will start by pulling the information directly from your resume. Start with what school[s] you have attended and the diploma or degree you have obtained or anticipate obtaining. Then, include any extracurricular clubs or organizations you are a part of underneath the "Activities and Societies" section.

Furthermore, include any minors, concentrations, or grade point averages under the "Description" section. You may wish to discuss your academic experience within the description; you are welcome to do so, but it is not required.

You may feel inclined to add courses you are taking, but you can relocate those into a separate "Course" section through the "Add Sections" button.

California Baptist University
Bachelor of Arts, Political Science
Sep 2021 - Dec 2025

Grade: Junior

Activities and societies: Integrated Single-Subject Credential Program | Student Senate | Alpha Chi Honors Soci
| Accreditation Steering Committee

Concentration: American Institutions and Processes
GPA: 3.98

Building Your LinkedIn

Experience Section. The following essential section is your "Experience." Similar to the About Section, you still want to tell a story. Do not just copy and paste your resume into this section; be detailed in your descriptions so that you give insights beyond the scope of the resume. Share stories, examples, and evidence of the skillset you have. This can be **task-oriented**, where you focus on "this is what I did, and here's how I did it." This can also be **story-driven**, where you focus on challenges, strengths, and growth gained through the experience. The key is to make sure you highlight both hard and soft skills necessary to your prospective industry.

Kids Camp Coach
FitOne Foundation · Contract
Aug 2020 - Aug 2022 · 2 yrs 1 mo
Riverside, California, United States

In this position I assist a non-profit organization, FitOne Foundation, a few times a year to put on free children's fitness camps. These camps usually are a weekend during each season of the year, and in 2020 we did a 12 week after-school program to get children moving and playing outside after sitting at home on the computer during the COVID-19 pandemic.

My responsibilities in the foundation are to assist the owners in planning and executing the camps. I act as a coach and teach the functional movements of Cross-fit to ages 5-12. Also on the days where we are not out in the park or hosting a camp, I operate as an administrative assistant and take inventory and data collection on the foundation's collections and expenses. I also brainstorm the events, fundraisers, and activities that the foundation holds.

Experience Section Model

LinkedIn allows you to expand on your experiences in ways you cannot on a resume. Capitalize on that ability by reflecting on your experiences and writing about them using a **first-person narrative**. Give employers and recruiters more details about who you are and what you have accomplished in writing that is more personalized than the facts on your resume.

Task-Oriented Experience

Task-oriented experience is similar to an expanded resume. Your resume bullet points that you workshopped on page 30 act as the skeleton for this model. Think about what you have done, how you did it, and why it matters to the organization you are working for.

Story-Driven Experience

Story-driven experience is where you can hone in on one aspect of your role. This is often more effective in leadership or project-based roles. Writing your experience through a story-driven lens relies on you reflecting on the challenges and growth you experienced through the experience rather than just describing the experience itself.

Look Ahead:

Story-driven experience is helpful when you prepare for an interview. You are adding personal insights into the position, rather than "this is what I did."

Experience Section Exercise

Build an outline for a task-oriented experience and a story-driven experience format for a singular position.

Past/Present Experience Title:

Task-Oriented Experience

For the above experience, return to the bullet points on your resume that you drafted, and brainstorm what you did and why you did it.

What did you do?

Try to write these in full sentences, in first person.

Why did you do it?

Story-Driven Experience

For the same experience, write a narrative highlighting what you did, but now focus on the growth and challenges you faced while working there. What did the growth and challenges reveal to you, and how did you improve?

Growth/Challenges:

Building Your LinkedIn

Additional Sections.

You can add the following additional sections from your resume to your LinkedIn profile:

- Skills
- Languages
- Licenses & Certifications
- Projects
- Posts
- Volunteer Experience
- Organizations
- Honors & Awards

"Have work evidence ready to go" (pg. 49) by posting about the projects you have been working on.

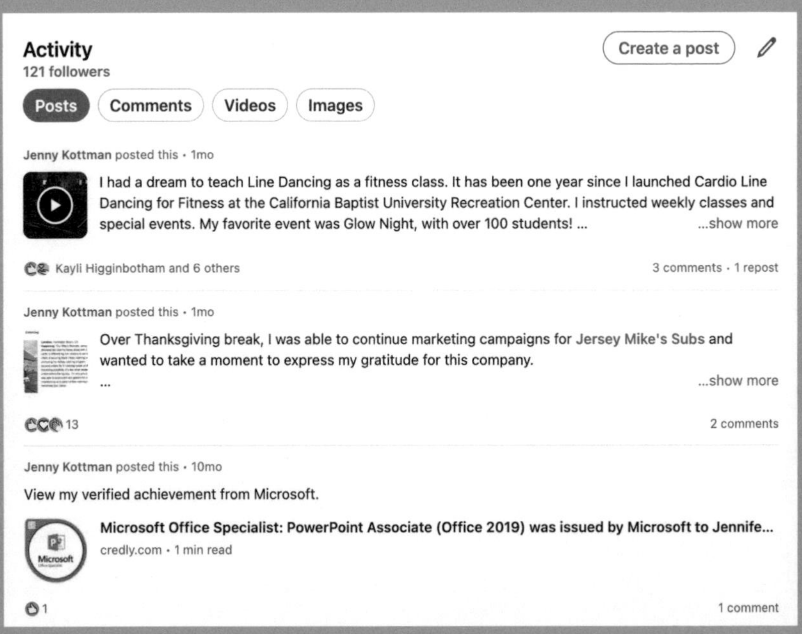

LinkedIn Checklist

This is the electronic and descriptive version of your resume. The categories are in the same order.

1 Visual Section:

- [ ] Headshot | Background photo
- [ ] Name | Tag line

2 About Section:

- [ ] "Tell me about you" ⟵ (past, present, future)

3 Education Section:

- [ ] Degree Title | School | Clubs | GPA

4 Experience Section:

- [ ] Resume bullets in sentence form
- [ ] Why those experiences were important
- [ ] Specific metrics ⟵ task oriented or story-driven

5 Additional Sections:

- [ ] Languages | Licenses & Certifications
- [ ] Projects [Work experience ready to go]
- [ ] Volunteer | Skills | Organizations | Awards

Building Your Network

Online Networking. Online networking does not lose any value simply because it only occurs online. These connections you make on platforms like LinkedIn are just as crucial as in-person professional relationships.

The internet is often a great way to stay in contact with those you do not get to network with frequently. Some great things to keep in mind when interacting with recruiters, employers, professionals, and alums in your field are:

- Getting connected on LinkedIn and other forms of media
- Keeping in touch through LinkedIn, whether it be DMs or comment sections on posts
- Cheering them on through any new achievements they share
- Asking questions and setting up informational interviews about the company or industry

Building Your Network

Organic Networking. Networking is not always easy to define. You may think of it as professional conferences and the internet connections used on LinkedIn. It is essential to realize that forming a network can also happen organically if you **intentionally form relationships** with the people you naturally cross paths with in person. Your classmates, teachers, coworkers, teammates, and community members you see daily are part of your network.

Listen to their stories, passions, hopes, and skills. Be a part of their journey, and help them if you can. The most "connected networkers" form relationships with everyone in their life. This information, opportunity, and expertise support system will be formed organically.

Maintaining Your Network

Saying "thank you." Thank you notes are a great follow-up for any interaction. This can take multiple forms. The best would be a **handwritten letter** that you can give to the receptionist or office administrator after an interview. Stop by the dollar store before you have an interview, grab a card, and put it in your car. After your interview, run out to the car and write out how/why you are thankful for the opportunity. Share something you are glad to have learned about their company through the interview. Thank them for their time as well. Do this even if the interview is virtual, except you'll **email** the interviewers directly. This may mean you need to ask them for their email address, or you can send it to the email that sent you the virtual link.

Network Maintenance. Do not neglect network maintenance. Just because you have a network does not mean they will always be there for you. You'll need to maintain frequent, yet not bothersome, contact with your network. A great way of doing this is by keeping milestone information and reaching out monthly or bimonthly to your network.

A thank you note is a great way to begin the back-and-forth connection by thanking your connection for their time, the opportunity, the conversation, or the interview. You establish the first point of contact.

From there, you can use the table on the next page or create a spreadsheet similar to the one you use to keep in contact with your network.

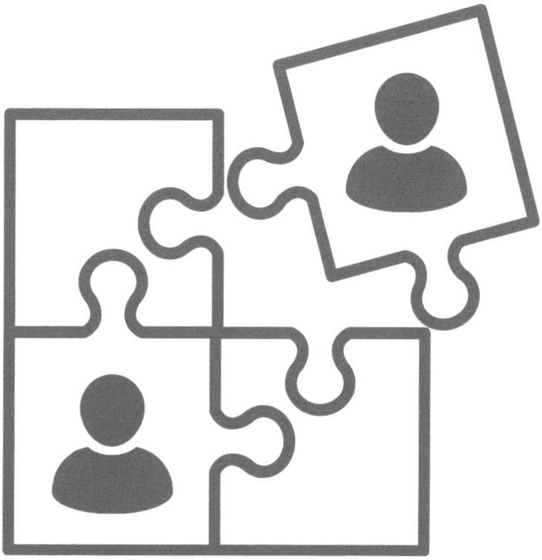

Networking Contact Table

Fill the table below out with information for your contacts so that you can stay in touch with them and set dates for you to reach out to them consistently.

Contact Name	Company	Position
John Smith	ABS Accounting	Talent Acquisition

Networking Contact Table

Set a contact frequency to help gauge how often you want to contact this network member. This chart is designed to help you stay accountable for your network maintenance.

Contact Info	Date Connected	Contact
jsmith@absaccount.com	August 10, 2024	90 days

Getting Connected. Networking is no easy task; it requires hard work and dedication to consistently build and create an active network.

You have made strides toward these steps throughout this chapter. Remember to stay on top of your network and continue growing it using online resources and organic connections.

Reach out to your network consistently. Just because you may not be actively looking for new positions does not make your network any less valuable.

You built a LinkedIn!
You built a network!
You are maintaining your network!

Connection

Allocation

The Fourth Piece

Everyone spends their time & money.
Few people spend it on what they actually want.

Allocation is spending a resource. In this case, we are looking at allocating your time and money. Allocating your time means giving your time to schedule commitments. Allocating your money means paying for things. You only have so much time and money, so you should see them both based on what has value to you.

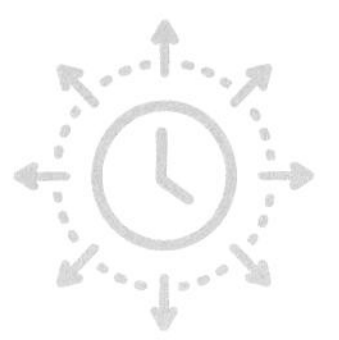

Allocation

Determining how you want to spend your time and money can be overwhelming. But it has a few simple components.

Start with the question:
1]"What is a valuable use of your time?" and examine your opportunity cost and priorities you have.

The second question is:
2]"What is a valuable use of your money?" This is helpful to assess how much money you make, what your life costs, and what you have left over to play with!

Ask yourself along the way:
3]"Are you allocating your time and money to prepare yourself for the direction you dreamed about in the first chapter?"

Time Allocation

Opportunity Cost is a critical concept to be aware of as you allocate your time. The basic idea is that your time has worth and earning potential. Everything you put your time towards takes away from an alternative potential opportunity you could have put your time towards. So, every “yes” to something is a “no” to other opportunities. We calculate the “cost” of those lost opportunities to decide how to spend our time. Doing everything is exhausting. Doing everything and expecting yourself to do them all well is not possible. So you need to pick what to spend your time on.

What opportunity could you pursue if you had more time?

What holds you back?

Time Allocation

Priorities. Fitting your commitments in your schedule is like trying to fit items in a glass jar. If you start with the sand, pebbles, and rocks, everything won't fit. If you put the rocks in first, then pebbles and sand, they will all fit. Establishing priorities is the critical decision of what to do with your time. Decide what is important to you. Put that in your schedule first [rocks].

Then, fill in the commitments of medium importance [pebbles].

Lastly, everything else [sand].

Time Allocation

What are the big rocks you want to prioritize in your schedule?

These are your most important commitments

✦
✦
✦
✦
✦

What are the pebbles that have medium importance in your schedule?

These are your secondary commitments

✦
✦
✦
✦
✦

What is the sand that will fill in the leftover space in your schedule?

These are the fun activities that fill your free time

✦
✦
✦

Time Allocation

Schedule. Keep track of your time commitments by creating a list of places to be and things to be completed in your calendar. You can keep a weekly or monthly calendar on paper. You can also utilize online platforms such as Google Calendar, Outlook Calendar, or the calendar app on your phone. Form ‘to do’ lists in your Notes app, Reminders app, Google Keep, or a paper to-do list. You’ve got this!

Just pick a system that works for you and stick with it! If you don‘t have one, try this! Fill in what you *have* to be at this week. Then, fill in what you *want* to be at this week.

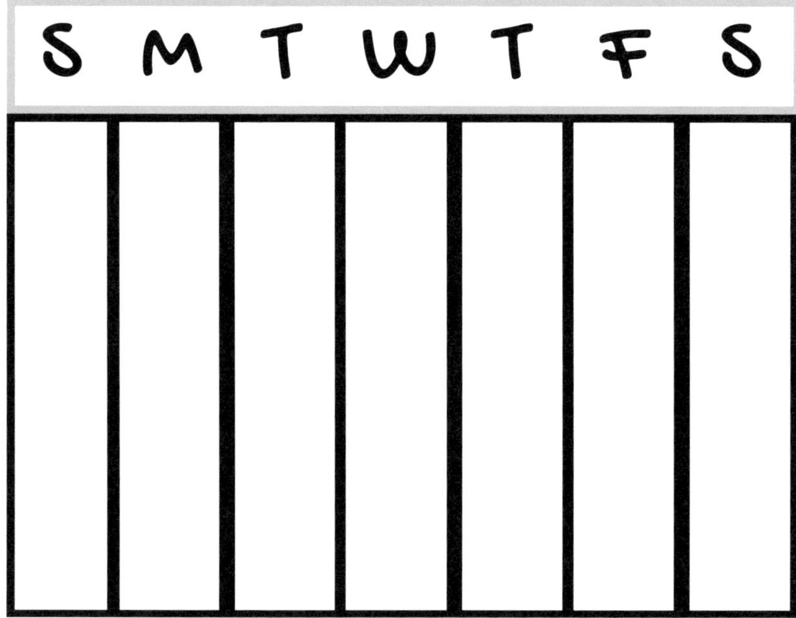

Money Allocation

Budgeting can seem overwhelming. But the basic idea is just knowing what your life costs [expenses] and making sure you earn enough money [income] to fund it.

Income: What You Made

- Part-time wage
- Full-time salary
- Side hustles
- Allowance

- Expenses: What Your Life Costs

- Debt [student/credit card]
- Housing [rent, mortgage]
- Transportation: Car [maintenance, payments, gas]
- Food [groceries, eating out, coffee]
- Phone
- Utilities
- Health [insurance]
- Membership [subscriptions, gym]

Money Left Over: Fun Money

- Entertainment [activities, lifestyle, travel]
- Save - Emergency fund [3-6 months of expenses]
- Gifts [giving]
- Invest [Retirement, Roth IRA, CDs, Mutual Fund]

Money Allocation

Income: What You Made!

________________________________ $______

________________________________ $______

________________________________ $______

Total Monthly Income **$______**

Sum of all your income

Expenses: What Your Life Costs

________________________________ $______

________________________________ $______

________________________________ $______

________________________________ $______

________________________________ $______

________________________________ $______

________________________________ $______

________________________________ $______

________________________________ $______

________________________________ $______

________________________________ $______

________________________________ $______

Total Monthly Expenses **$______**

Sum of all your expenses

Subtract

Money Left Over: **$______**

If this is a <u>positive number</u>, great! You made more than you spent and can play! If this is a <u>negative number</u>, be careful. You are spending more than you make. To fix this, you need to buy less or make more.

Time and Money. These are your critical resources. They are the pinnacle of your work and personal life. Learning how to allocate these resources properly is essential to your functioning as a professional and human being.

The sooner you learn time and budget management, the easier it becomes to develop yourself in the working world. Developing these habits will help you reach the destination you dreamed of on page 21.

Your time is valuable!
Your money is valuable!
Use it to head in the right direction!

Allocation

Puzzle Progress

Career paths feel like a **puzzle,** but you put the **pieces together,** and can fill in the **whole picture.**

Joshua 1:9

Made in United States
Troutdale, OR
09/19/2024